GW00702737

Book 2

Ten enjoyable pieces arranged by
Adrian Vernon Fish

kevin
mayhew

kevin mayhew

First published in Great Britain in 1993 by Kevin Mayhew Ltd
Tel: +44 (0) 1449 737978

www.kevinmayhew.com

© Copyright 1993 Kevin Mayhew Ltd.

ISBN 0 86209 357 0
Catalogue No. 3611088

1 2 3 4 5 6 7 8 9

All or part of these pieces have been arranged by Adrian Vernon Fish
and are the copyright of Kevin Mayhew Ltd.

Cover design: Sara-Jane Came
Music Editor: Anthea Smith

Printed and bound in Great Britain

Contents

ADRIAN VERNON FISH (b.1956), who selected and arranged the music in this book, is a composer, organist and harpsichordist. He studied at the Royal College of Music in London under Herbert Howells, Alan Ridout, Nicholas Danby, Joseph Horovitz and Ruth Dyson.

He composes in most forms, from symphonies to cabaret songs.

ALLEGRETTO

Paolo Tosti (1846 - 1916)

Con tenerezza

7

THE BLACKBIRD

Fred Weatherly (1849 - 1929)

9

FUNERAL MARCH

Niels Gade (1817 - 1890)

PRELUDE

Alexander Scriabin (1872 - 1915)

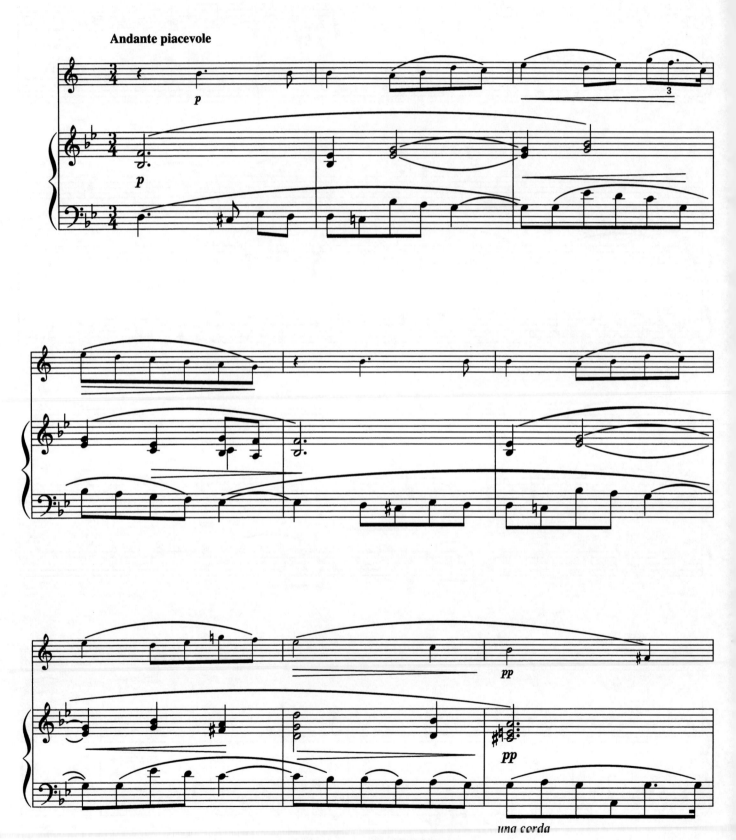

DREAMING

Robert Schumann (1810 - 1856)

TO A WILD ROSE

Edward MacDowell (1860 - 1908)

With simple tenderness

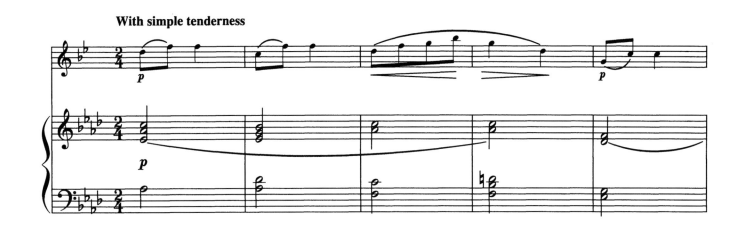

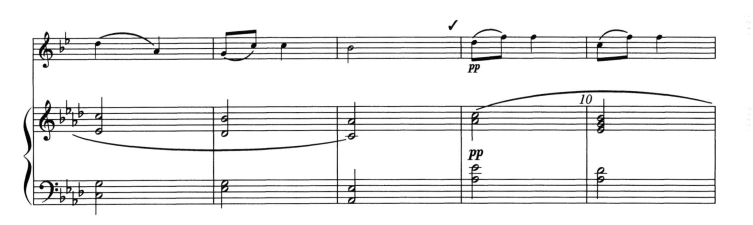

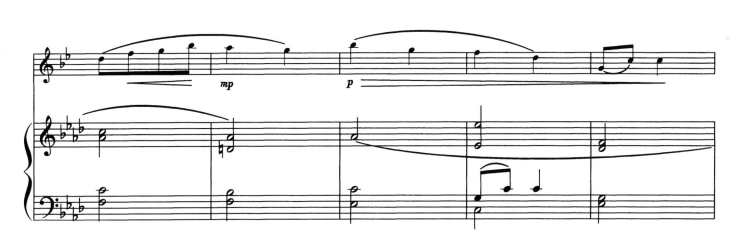

SOLVEJG'S SONG

Edvard Grieg (1843 - 1907)

Carnival for Clarinet

Book 2

Ten enjoyable pieces arranged by
Adrian Vernon Fish

kevin
mayhew

ALLEGRETTO

Paolo Tosti (1846 - 1916)

THE BLACKBIRD

Fred Weatherly (1849 - 1929)

FUNERAL MARCH

Niels Gade (1817 - 1890)

PRELUDE

Alexander Scriabin (1872 - 1915)

DREAMING

Robert Schumann (1810 - 1856)

TO A WILD ROSE

Edward MacDowell (1860 - 1908)

SOLVEJG'S SONG

Edvard Grieg (1843 - 1907)

9

LARGHETTO PASTORALE

Samuel Wesley (1766 - 1837)

LIED

Heinrich Hofmann (1842 - 1902)

THE GUARDIAN ANGEL

Liza Lehmann (1862 - 1918)

Allegretto con moto

LARGHETTO PASTORALE

Samuel Wesley (1766 - 1837)

LIED

Heinrich Hofmann (1842 - 1902)

29

THE GUARDIAN ANGEL

Liza Lehmann (1862 - 1918)

Moderato

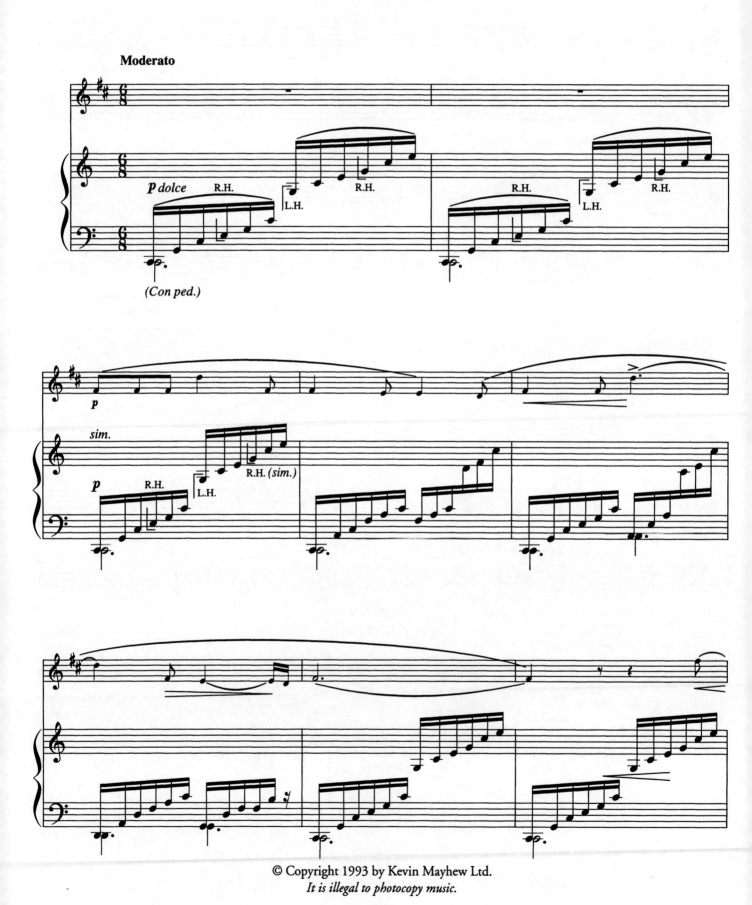

31